Online News Recommendation Systems in Machine Learning

Bibliographic information published by the German National Library:

The German National Library lists this publication in the National Bibliography; detailed bibliographic data are available on the Internet at http://dnb.dnb.de.

ISBN: 9783346820839
This book is also available as an ebook.

© GRIN Publishing GmbH
Nymphenburger Straße 86
80636 München

Print and binding: Books on Demand GmbH, Norderstedt, Germany
Printed on acid-free paper from responsible sources.

The present work has been carefully prepared. Nevertheless, authors and publishers do not incur liability for the correctness of information, notes, links and advice as well as any printing errors.

GRIN web shop: https://www.grin.com/document/1325265

Online News Recommendation System

Table of Contents

Abstract

Online news reading has gained more attention in recent years than ever, particularly based on the increasing dependence of users on smartphones and the internet. Leading a busy lifestyle, end-users find it hard to search for relevant news articles online, and require tools that could provide them with the most needed news feed on the go. Although legacy news recommendation systems do exist, yet they do not offer optimum efficiency and accuracy. Bearing in mind the increasing need for access to personalized news, the current research study aims at developing an online news recommendation system that could offer an optimum online news reading experience in a highly personalized fashion. The study considers major methodologies and perspectives, such as reinforced learning, Q-Learning, Collaborative Filtering and User Profiling, within this domain in order to implement the ONRS system.

Keywords: Content Filtering; Reinforcement Learning; User Profiling.

3

Context

Traditionally, news retrieval was exclusively limited to paper, which also made it highly localized and restricted. However, with the passage of time and the development of the World Wide Web, inter-continental news retrieval started to become more convenient than ever. This abrupt change opened new opportunities while expanding the boundaries for the traditional news reporting agencies (Das et al, 2007; Xu et al, 2015). A direct outcome of the increased adoption and reliance of the internet among the masses was the development of online news platforms that tend to provide individuals with news feed that is highly in demand (Li et al, 2011; Hopfgartner et al, 2016). However, these agencies still struggle with content filtering and provisioning, which is mainly because of the significant differences between personal traits, likes and interests (Liu, Dolan & Pedersen, 2010). This eventually led to the development of online news recommendation systems that could potentially help overcome this barrier (Elkahky et al, 2015). However, despite considerable efforts, an optimal solution with this regard is yet to be developed. In essence, the main source of content filtering in traditional news recommender systems is the individual or user behavior and the respective preferences (Liang et al, 2006). Nonetheless, one major problem with the traditional news recommendation systems is that they fail to focus on the individual needs and preferences, while treating users as a whole (Hopfgartner et al, 2014). As such, many of the news recommendation systems that make use of content filtering utilize the one-size-fits-all approach, which is non-compliant with the individual needs of the present day (Hung, 2005). Many recent research studies render the traditional news recommendation systems incompetent, as they derive new and improved algorithms from the ones previously proposed (Garcin et al, 2014; Lu et al, 2015). Based on these patterns, an opportunity to potentially propose a more efficient and accurate online news recommendation system has been identified. Hence, this research study aims to build on the recently completed research studies and their respective outcomes in order to implement an enhanced version of the recommender system that takes into account the major prerequisites.

Widespread penetration of the World Wide Web coupled with the internet is quite evident. Contemporary Information and Communication Technologies are paving new pathways to conduct daily life activities more efficiently and conveniently. Among other rising trends, one prominent trend to note is the vast utilization of online information channels and platforms to retrieve news about the latest events. Thanks to Web 2.0 accompanied by lightning fast internet access, users across the globe are now able to retrieve and skim through the most in-demand news articles right from the comfort of their smartphones or other handheld devices. Not to mention, the development of the smart technologies, driven by smartphones, smart watches and tablet Personal Computers has further eased and promoted access to the most updated information.

However, with the increasing development of new and enhanced online news platforms, a major barrier today is the availability of personalized news. Not all users can be expected to have advance level knowledge of the computing domain, which is why it is important to come up with solutions that can facilitate in provision of highly personalized news articles. This would require the system to be able to constantly monitor and evaluate user searches made on a frequent basis, which could provide insights into user likes and interests. Consequently, the system needs to be able to provide access to preferential news articles based on the user's recent searches and views. The purpose of this dissertation is to implement an online news recommendation system, given the alias ONRS, which solves this barrier by providing the most user-specific news. ONRS would make use of user-specific information available across social media and general searches that a user makes through the Google search engine. The ONRS would gather and interpret this data into valuable information so as to identify, collect and present the most desired news articles to the end-user. The ONRS system would be implemented by virtue of a web interface with user friendly visualizations in order to feed the end-user with latest and filtered news feed. The online news recommendation system would integrate aspects of several computational techniques, including machine learning, clustering, user modeling / profiling and collaborative filtering in order to succeed in provision of the news articles based on user end-user preferences.

Since social media networks serve as the go-to point for accessing highly personalized and user-specific information, it is highly viable to make use of information available across these platforms as data sources for the proposed ONRS system. As such, the ONRS system would make use of two main types of feedback, including explicit feedback and implicit feedback from the end-user to serve the central purpose of providing personalized and preferred online news articles. Explicit feedback would require the end-user to directly engage with the ONRS web interface to set news preferences, whereas implicit feedback would utilize user-specific information gathered from the analysis of user-specific information gathered from social media. For example, implicit feedback from Facebook would include identification of user's likes, reactions, interests and views.

Motivation

End-user demands and preferences with regards to digital content differs significantly, similar to any other area of interest. The central motivation for this dissertation came from the pertinent lack of a highly effective and efficient recommendation system that could offer the end-users with highly specific and preferred information. Preliminary research helped in identifying only a handful of recommendation systems that had been developed in the recent past. However, a major downside of these recommendation systems was that none of them were further developed. Instead, each recommendation system appeared as a stand-alone solution that needs significant work. Thus, in order for a recommendation system to really work, it is important to consider the prevailing gaps and weaknesses, and come up with a more effective solution that holds significant potential for future research and development. In addition to lack of appropriate research and development, another drawback of the existing recommendation systems proposed on paper is that they do not integrate the techniques of machine learning and clustering. Bearing in mind the widespread utilization, high accuracy and efficiency of machine learning and clustering techniques, it is highly desirable to leverage their potential in developing more enhanced news recommendation systems that save time and effort, while providing user-specific content. By doing so, the online news recommendation system aims at satisfying user needs and requirements for access to appropriate content on demand.

Furthermore, the research team feels highly motivated to make optimum use of the widely available sources of information, some of which provide highly useful insights on a range of subjects and areas of discussion. Retrospect is suggestive of the presence of a multitude of information sources that can serve as data-hubs; however, in its current state, end-users have to put in significant time and effort in order to search, identify and retrieve the required information. Most of the times, due to lack of knowledge, a majority of online news readers miss out on the ness articles and content that could have proved essential. For example, most Information Technology researchers and enthusiasts tend to search for the latest news, events and happening online. For some, this information may prove useful in development of their personal research projects that could aid in the development or refinement of broader technological solutions. End-users of online news sources may be in search of new information, or information that may inspire the development of new solutions. Hence, it is of utmost significance to come up with an effective solution that makes sure that readers never miss out on the news of interest, and make the most out of their time reading through the various articles of interest. Completion of this research study would extend the availability of literature, while experiencing new possibilities in developing more enhanced online news recommendation systems. This would also motivate future researchers in extending the current research work and potentially develop large-scale solutions.

Structure

The rest of this paper has been organized as follows;

- Chapter 2 – State of the Art: This chapter is aimed at gathering and reporting on contextual information with regards to online news recommendation systems, machine learning, clustering and other important methodologies. The chapter provides retrospective information on the online news recommendation systems currently available, and on key methodologies, such as Reinforced Learning Algorithms, QLearning, user modeling and adaptive user profiling, and collaborative filtering. The chapter also covers related work completed in the field of online news recommendation and content filtering systems.

- Chapter 3 – Proposed Solution: This chapter provides an in-depth description of the proposed solution, which is the ONRS online news recommendation system. It provides information on the main data sources for the ONRS system, the methodologies that will be applied for the ONRS system to function appropriately, and the methods for evaluation of results / research outcomes.

- Chapter 4 – Planning: This chapter is aimed at reflecting on the research plan, with information on the research aims, objectives, timeframe and resources required for successful completion of the project.

- Chapter 5 – Conclusion: This chapter draws on the entire research paper, and provides appropriate conclusions with regards to state of the art, methodologies and related work and available solutions. The chapter also provides concluding remarks on the proposed solution, and how it compares to the already available news

recommendation systems.

Chapter 2: State of the Art

2.1. Methodologies

2.1.1. Methodology 1 – Reinforcement Learning

There is a substantial body of literature available that speaks of the various

methodologies applicable to recommendation systems. To begin with, Reinforced Learning is

a technique that has received significant attention from the research community mainly

because of its unique capability to foster learning without the need of a teacher. In other

words, it is an experimentation-based learning where there is no requirement for a teacher to

demonstrate practical examples for learning to occur (Ribeiro, 1999). Experience plays the

role of the teacher in Reinforced Learning techniques. Due to this unique experience-driven

learning capability, Reinforced Learning is applicable across a vast variety of fields,

including robotics and operational research domains. However, review of retrospect only

revealed historic research within the domain of Reinforcement Learning, showing that this

technique has not received much attention in recent times (Lauer & Riedmiller, 2000;

Brafman & Tennenholtz, 2002). Absence of more recent research studies on the application

and use of Reinforced Learning techniques does not mean that RL techniques can be deemed

irrelevant or ineffective. In fact, a range of reinforcement learning algorithms have been

developed and tested in the past, while also being proven highly effective in a variety of

ways. Exploring the various applications of reinforcement learning techniques would make

the current research scope too broad in nature, hence this study exclusively focuses on the

potential role of reinforcement learning in developing news recommendation systems.

Literature shows that Reinforcement Learning techniques are facilitated by a

specialized reinforcement learning agent, which can play a range of roles (Ribeiro, 1999).

However, the agent that is applicable to the research topic under study is the one described by

Lin (1991). He described reinforcement learning agent as a self-improving reactive agent that learns and develops with experience (Lin, 1991; Russell & Norvig, 1995). As described earlier, the central principle of the online news recommendation system is to provide end-users with more relevant news content by skimming through the explicit and implicit feedback provided by the user himself. This shows that the online news recommendation system resembles the Reinforcement Learning agent described by Lin (1991), improving its capability to filter and personalize news content with experience through passage of time. This situation can be explained by considering an example scenario where the end-user 'A' is highly motivated towards staying abreast of the latest trends in the smartphone industry. More frequently, the user searches for top smartphones, smartphone processors, mobile camera technologies and operating systems by making use of multiple online sources, including but not limited to Facebook, Google Search and news feed such as XDA Feed. However, the user has to put in considerable time and effort in order to manually search and read the required news articles. By implementing the Reinforcement Learning agent to develop the recommendation system, the end-user 'A' will be able to receive the latest updates automatically.

The Reinforcement Learning (RL) agent plays a reactive role by making use of an action policy that is created after carefully observing and mapping the user actions, internal conditions of the system and readily available information (Ribeiro, 1999). The direct outcome of this reactive process is new learning and the process continues over time. For RL agent to be effective in the implementation of an online news recommendation system, the agent must be able to self-improve through experience in the absence of a teacher (Ribeiro, 1999). As such, the agent must make use of its interactions with the end user's search queries in order to acquire learning. Reinforcement Learning can therefore be implemented in the form of a self-improving process in order to make the ONRS system more effective and powerful.

2.1.2. Methodology 2 – Q-Learning

Perhaps a more effective form of Reinforcement Learning algorithms is Q-Learning, which can be characterized as an off-policy algorithm (CSE, 2018). It is a specialized Reinforcement Learning technique that is model-free in essence (Hu & Wellman, 2003). Q-Learning algorithms have been applied to determine the optimal action-selection policy, working by learning an action-value function (Greenwald et al, 2003). The Q-learning algorithm model comprises of two main components, including an agent and a state S along with a set of actions per state A (Greenwald et al, 2003). As such, the Q-Learning agent gains the capability of transitioning from one state to another by virtue of a specific action that results in the generation of a reward for the agent (Greenwald et al, 2003). The central motive of the Q-Learning agent is the maximization of rewards by moving from state to state, while also learning new information as it goes along a specific path (Greenwald et al, 2003). Rewards maximization and sequential learning is directly linked with the proposed solution of a recommendation system, which provides even improved news results with the passage of time.

To build a contextual background of the Q-Learning methodology, the study conducted by Gambardella & Dorigo (1995) where the Ant-Q methodology, a primitive variant of the Q-Learning methodology, was proposed by making use of the traditional Q-Learning methodology proposed by Watkins in 1980 (Gambardella & Dorigo, 1995). Although their study takes into account the Travelling Salesman Problem (TSP), yet it can be considered to build a basic understanding of how Q-Learning methodologies can be modified. The Ant-Q algorithm undergoes combinatorial optimization inspired by the Ant colonies and their activities. The researchers practically demonstrate the implementation of the Ant-Q algorithm to achieve more effective outcomes on symmetric TSPs (Gambardella & Dorigo, 1995). Thus, the Ant-Q algorithm as proposed by Gambardella & Dorigo (1995) can be considered in the limelight of distributed algorithms as a means of achieving combinatorial optimizations. To be specific, the combinatorial optimizations through Ant-Q can be applied for combining external and internal feedback to optimize the news feed on the proposed ONRS system. The central concept of the Ant-Q variant is that ant colonies and their respective behaviors can be mimicked in order to determine the shortest article search queries within optimal time periods.

Shixiang et al (2016) have proposed a more enhanced version of the Q-Learning methodology, which makes it more opportune to consider it for the subsequent development of the proposed system. They point out one major limitation with the model-free reinforcement learning techniques, which is a greater degree of sample complexity, specifically with the case of high-dimensional functional approximators (Shixiang et al, 2016). In a successful attempt to overcome this sample complexity, the researchers proposed two complementary methodologies that have substantially improved the overall efficiency of the traditional model-free Q-Learning algorithms (Shixiang et al, 2016). To begin with, they derived and presented a continuous variant of the Q-Learning algorithm identified as NAF or Normalized Advantage Function (Shixiang et al, 2016). The NAF function serves as an effective substitute to the policy gradient methods that are traditionally used in Q-Learning (Shixiang et al, 2016). According to the researchers, this transition enabled them to apply Q-Learning with experience replay to continuous tasks (Shixiang et al, 2016). In the context of the proposed research study, this variant of the Q-Learning methodology could potentially prove useful in improving the overall efficacy of the ONRS system through enhanced experience replay on continuously browsed news articles across a wide variety of end-users. The researchers managed to further improve the efficiency of the system by implementing the learned models for acceleration of model-free Q-Learning methodology (Shixiang et al, 2016).

The research study conducted by Hasslet, Guez & Silver (2016) made use of a different approach altogether. Their study proposes a double Q-Learning as a variant of the deep reinforcement learning family (Hasslet, Guez & Silver, 2016). Their study makes use of the DQN algorithm – a unique algorithm that integrates deep neural networks and Q-Learning – while also bearing in mind its key limitation of overestimating in various domains (Hasslet, Guez & Silver, 2016). The study proposes generalized utilization of the Double Q-Learning algorithm in order to achieve large-scale functional approximations (Hasslet, Guez & Silver, 2016). A thorough review of their research study shows that the problem of sequential decisions can be best solved by virtue of optimal estimates for each action (Hasslet, Guez & Silver, 2016). Although the algorithms explained and derived as part of this study are quite comprehensive to be included in this paper, yet it is viable to state that the Double Q-Learning variant of the Q-Learning methodology can be applied to the ONRS system being proposed here. Implementation of this variant holds value as it may ensure the achievement of optimal approximation, thereby enabling the ONRS system to provide highly personalized news articles to the prospective readers.

2.1.3. Methodology 3 – Collaborative User Feedback

Another noteworthy methodology that is of direct relevance to the current research study is that of Collaborative User Feedback, as defined by Agrawal and colleagues (2009). It was highlighted earlier that the proposed Online News Recommendation System plans to make use of both explicit and implicit user feedback in order to perform the job of providing filtered and personalized news content. This explicit and implicit feedback is jointly recognized as Collaborative User Feedback, and is aimed at improving the overall accuracy and efficiency of the proposed ONRS system (Agrawal et al, 2009). Equation 1 shared below represents both explicit and implicit feedback;

$$F = \{(u_i, a_j, f_{ij})\} \ldots \ldots \text{Eq. } 1$$

In the above equation, u represents the user, a represents the article and f represents both explicit and implicit user feedback (Agrawal et al, 2009). For the proposed ONRS system, Collaborative User Feedback will be collected in three ways, including click-through, rating and recommendation (Agrawal et al, 2009). Thus, the f in equation 1 represents these three types of feedback, thereby utilizing information from the feedback in order to provide more accurate and personalized news articles to the end users. The research study conducted by Chechev & Koychev (2014) builds on the study results of Agarwal et al (2009) to propose an Collaborative Feedback based news recommender system that analyzes and filters search results from Facebook. Their research study contends that the contemporary internet users do not prefer to make use of complex methodologies in order to manually find the desired news articles, and instead require a system that could automatically take input from the end-users while they are using the social network – Facebook in this case – in order to provide the most desired and interesting new articles (Chechev & Koychev, 2014). Their study is suggestive of the need for developing a custom news feed application based on Collaborative User Feedback in order to offer a highly personalized user experience (Chechev & Koychev, 2014).

Perhaps a more enhanced version of the Collaborative User Feedback methodology is the one presented by Shahmohammadi et al (2016). They have implemented the collaborative filtering methods as a means of achieving and securing collaborative user feedback (Shahmohammadi et al, 2016). The researchers have proposed collaborative path as a new version of collaborative user feedback, based on which a total of four directed proximity

15

measures have been proposed alongside three new algorithms (Shahmohammadi et al, 2016). Two of these algorithms have been based on the collaborative random walks for multilayer network and mixed network respectively (Shahmohammadi et al, 2016). Additionally, the authors have also proposed the Collaborative-Association-Rule algorithm (Shahmohammadi et al, 2016). By putting collaborative user data retrieved from Facebook to use, the authors clearly demonstrate that the cold-start problem can actively be avoided, while more enhanced activity prediction could be achieved at the same time (Shahmohammadi et al, 2016). Results and recommendations from this research study can be utilized in order to further refine the proposed ONRS system, integrating the use of Collaborative User Feedback algorithms to suggest relevant news articles based on the likes, posts, shares and comments of the collaborative users across the various social networks and online news sharing platforms (Shahmohammadi et al, 2016).

2.1.4. Methodology 4 – User Profile Construction

Yet another notable methodology that is applicable in the current case scenario is that of user profiling or user profile construction. Unlike the aforementioned methodologies, user profiling is somewhat simpler in essence. This technique involves monitoring and analysis of the history of an end-user's interests with regards to a particular subject area (Saranya & Sadhasivam, 2012). These user profiles can be categorized as either static or dynamic user profiles. Static user profiling involves the collection of information with regards to a user's likes or interests at the time of sign-up, or when the end-user initiates usage of a particular website or information source (Saranya & Sadhasivam, 2012). Static user profiles generally entail information regarding user interests, hobbies, work context or industry and usernames. On the other hand, dynamic user profiling is associated with determination of the changing likes or interests of users over a specified time period (Saranya & Sadhasivam, 2012). Dynamic user profiles can be constructed with the help of explicit interest indicators that are triggered during each interactive search session (Saranya & Sadhasivam, 2012). Dynamic user profiling makes use of data such as the recently accessed news content, repeated access patterns and categorization of the news articles accessed by a particular user. However, the system must be able to access the user's history in order to attain such data for user profiling. Bearing in mind the ethical principles of privacy and confidentiality, the end-users are given the privilege to allow or deny access to their usage history across all devices. Thus, the online news recommendation system must be developed such that it appears as a trustworthy platform for the end-users, so that they allow access to their personalized usage history to get improved results. The research study conducted by Liu, Dolan & Pedersen (2010) is also of prominence with regards to the user profiling methodology, as they proposed a personalized news recommendation system in Google News. Their proposed system makes use of the user profiles developed through the data retrieved from web history – depending on the fact that the users are logged into their individual accounts and have explicitly enabled web history – in order to facilitate the end users with the most desired news articles or content (Liu, Dolan & Pedersen, 2010). To sum up, their proposed system develops end-user profiles based on their recent click behaviors while going through online news feed (Liu, Dolan & Pedersen, 2010). The system aggregates the end-users' click logs and analyzes them to provide highly appropriate news content.

Another practical demonstration of the relative effectiveness of user profiling with regards to news recommendation is the study conducted by Pazzani & Billsus (2007), whereby a specialized contend-based news recommendation system has been proposed. They argue that despite the prevailing differences between the various content-based recommendation systems, there underlies a uniqueness, which is user profiling (Pazzani & Billsus, 2007). Their study is of particular significance because they consider a more theoretic approach and expand on the technique of user-profiling and how it works. They

17

define user profiling as the ability of a system to identify, evaluate and analyze the likes and interests of an end-user, thereby comparing the results in an ongoing fashion to offer personalized content feed (Pazzani & Billsus, 2007).

A technique that is closely linked with the User Profiling methodology that can potentially be utilized for the implementation of the proposed ONRS system is that of personalized filtering or personalized recommendations (Saranya & Sadhasivam, 2012). According to literature, this technique calculates the similarity between topic distributions of every news group and the usage history through adaptive profiling (Saranya & Sadhasivam, 2012). This requires direct engagement from the end-user, where queries can be posted through the recommendation frame after signing up with the ONRS system. Input of queries to the recommendation frame would generate a set of personalized results, while constantly updating the search behaviors through dynamic profiling, as explained earlier (Saranya & Sadhasivam, 2012). Personalized recommendation technique also gives the end-users the liberty to make explicit interactions with the system in order to update their respective likes and interests.

The use of Dynamic Updating Policy has also been identified in retrospect as an effective technique of adaptive user profiling. This technique largely makes use of the registration information provided by the end-user during the time of registration along with other user preferences recorded. Additionally, per-click computations are made where each click on a different category of news articles updates the click frequency by 1. Completion of such behavior leads to a complete update of the user-profile in an adaptive manner. This presents two case scenarios. First, the information and preferences explicitly provided by the user during registration is utilized for provision of personalized news articles and content. Second, every click on the various categories of news articles is recorded, and the user profile is updated in a continuous fashion. These two scenarios work collaboratively in a dynamic manner in order to keep providing more improved search results than before, making the technique ideal for implementation at the proposed ONRS system.

2.2. Related Work

2.2.1. News Recommendation System for Social Networks (Agarwal et al, 2009)

As identified earlier, a considerable degree of work has already been conducted in the domain of online news recommendation systems. Agarwal and colleagues (2009) have considered the use of social networking user data in order to develop and implement an online news recommendation system for social networks, where user-specific data from Facebook is utilized on a large scale. In accordance with the methodologies described earlier, their proposed system makes use of content-based recommendations through user-profiling in order to present personalized RSS feeds (Agarwal et al, 2009). The proposed recommendation system analyzes and uses three main types of user-specific data from Facebook, including clickthroughs of articles ($f1$), rating of articles ($f2$) and user-to-user article recommendations ($f3$) (Agarwal et al, 2009). Characterizing the articles and users as a_j and u_i, their recommendation system secures and integrates three types of user feedback (Agarwal et al, 2009). In addition to user profiling, their proposed system also makes use of the Collaborative User Feedback algorithm, as already described in earlier parts, in order to further improve the efficiency and accuracy of online news recommendation (Agarwal et al, 2009). The study presents use-cases, which makes it more convenient and clear to use the outcomes for the subsequent development of the proposed ONRS system.

2.2.2. Personalized Online News Recommendation System (Saranya, 2012)

Further review of literature helped in identifying the research study by Sarany & Sadhasivam (2012) where a personalized online news recommendation system based on adaptive user profiling and collaborative filtering has been proposed. The Adaptive User

Profiling approach has thoroughly been described as the means of news selection based on

intrinsic property of an end-user's interest presented at a particular point in time (Saranya &

Sadhasivam, 2012). The authors argue that Adaptive User Profiling helps in maintaining

equilibrium between novelty and diversity of news recommendations (Saranya &

Sadhasivam, 2012). In addition, the researchers show that Adaptive User Profiling capitalizes

over unique characteristics, such as the context of news, popularity of the news article and

patterns of access to news articles (Saranya & Sadhasivam, 2012). A complete news

recommendation framework that can serve as a major reference for the proposed ONRS

system has been presented below.

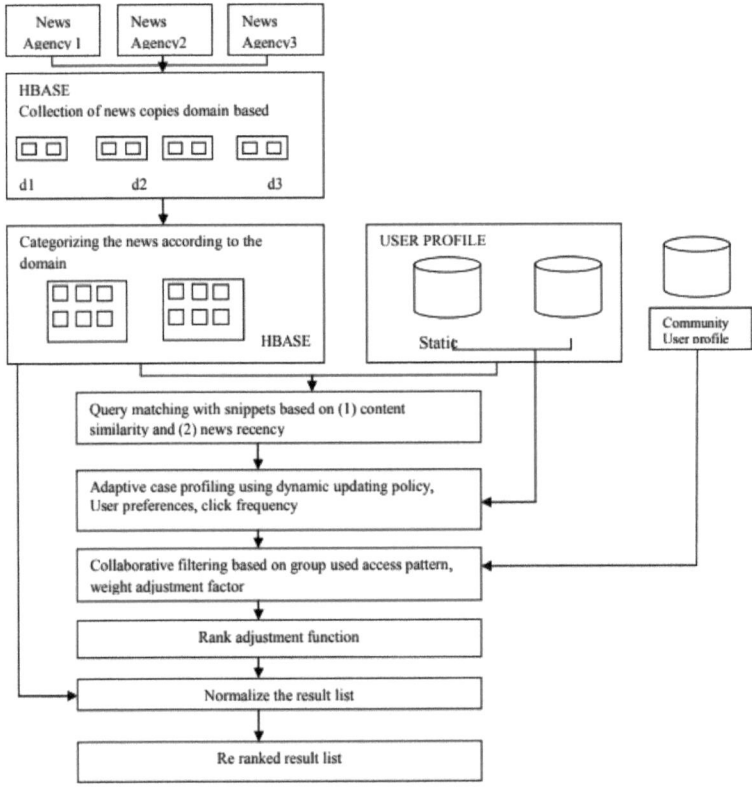

Figure 1 Proposed News Recommendation Framework (Saranya & Sadhasivam, 2012)

However, the main strength of this research study is that they also leverage the

Collaborative filtering approach in order to add value to the recommendation system. The

recommendation system characterizes user preferences as demonstrated in the below figure;

Row Key	User preference with in a particular domain					
	User name	Password	Working Context	Category 1 with its associated weight	Category 2 with its associated weight	Category n with its associated weight

Figure 2: User Preference Characterization (Saranya & Sadhasivam, 2012)

As such, the overall architecture of the online news recommendation system that can also prove relevant is shared in what follows;

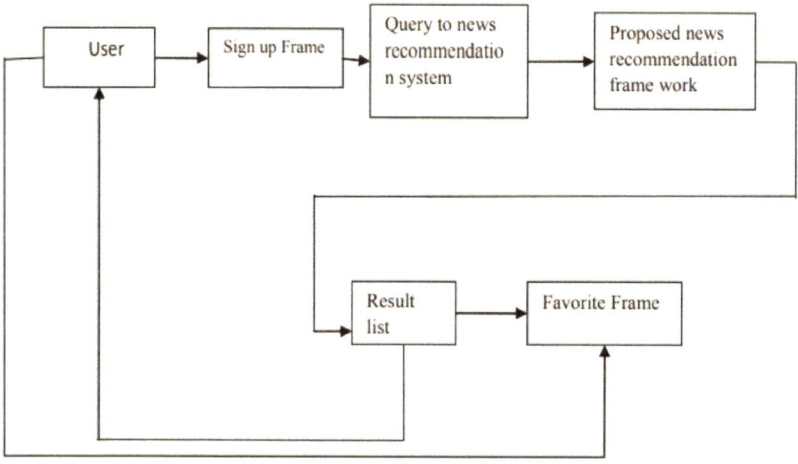

Figure 3 ONRS Architecture (Saranya & Sadhasivam, 2012)

It is important to note here that collaborative filtering has been considered influential in identifying, analyzing and recording user behavior specific to online content platforms (Das et al, 2007; Goldberg et al, 2001; Claypool & Gokhale, 1999). It is also important to note that the recommendation to combine collaborative filtering with user profiling has not received much attention from a practical / experimental perspective in recent times. Hence, the study by Saranya & Sadhasivam (2012) can be utilized as the only means of understanding the Adaptive User Profiling and Collaborative filtering techniques. It is anticipated that the implementation of a hybrid approach that combines multiple methodologies can assist in the development of the ONRS with expected performance attributes.

2.2.3. SCENE News Recommendation System (Li et al 2011)

The research study conducted by Li et al (2011) also adheres to a similar approach for news selection based on intrinsic property of an end-user's interest presented at a particular point in time (Saranya & Sadhasivam, 2012). However, their proposed system differs from the one proposed by Saranya & Sadhasivam (2012) in a sense that it adopts a scalable 2-stage personalized news recommendation system that has a two-level representation (Li et al, 2011). The approach proposed by Li et al (2011) leverages the exclusive characteristics, including access patterns, news content, article popularity and named entities in order to offer a personalized online news user experience (Li et al, 2011). The system proposed by Li et al (2011) considers the use of hierarchical clustering, content matching and similar cluster selection in order to put together an optimized news recommendation system (Merialdo, 1999; Fung et al, 2002), as shown below;

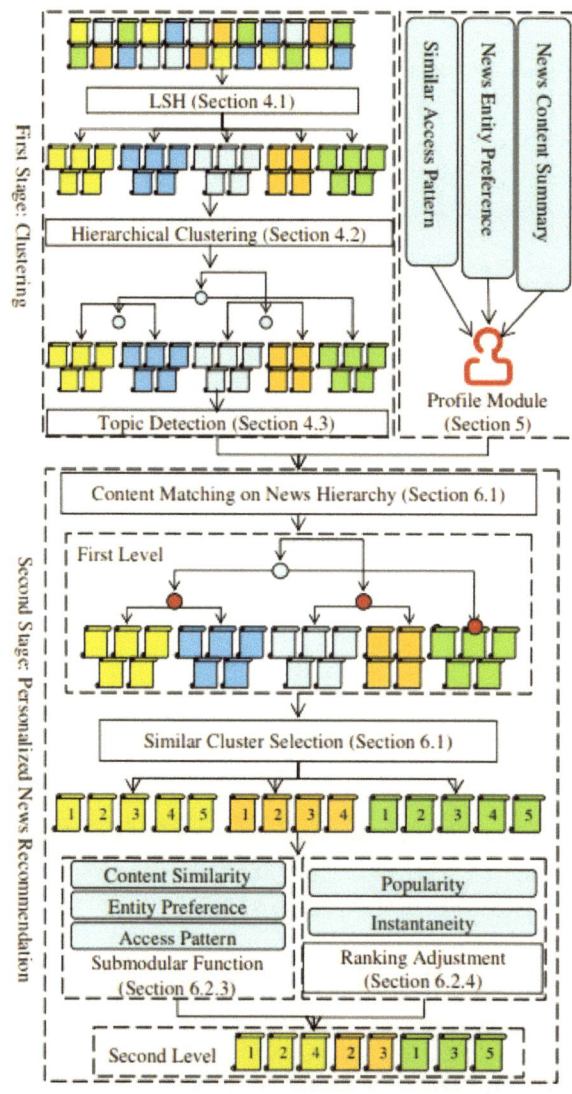

Figure 4 SCENE System Framework (Li et al, 2011)

Chapter 3: Work Plan

The proposed dissertation will follow a specific work plan as elaborated below;

Stage 1: Theory

The first stage of the work plan will be to develop a complete theoretical understanding of the main concepts, methodologies and techniques involved.

Stage 2: Proposal Development

The second stage would be to develop a dissertation proposal that is complete in all respects, and compliant with the requisites of a standard dissertation. This would involve the following activities;

- Initial meeting with the dissertation supervisor.
- Proposal submission requirements.
- Proposal outline.
- Complete literature review.
- Decision on research methodology.
- Proposal review and submission.

Stage 3: Proposal Defense and Further Research

The third stage would involve filing paperwork and scheduling proposal defense. Permission will be secured from the committee. After the proposal defense meet, the proposal will be reviewed and revised as necessary.

Stage 4: Dissertation Writing and Defense

The final stage would involve completion of the dissertation, which complies with the proposal submitted and approved. The following activities will be completed as part of this stage;

- Dissertation writing.
- Submission of the initial dissertation draft to the supervisor.
- Review and revision of the draft.
- Finalizing the dissertation.
- Proofreading and professionally presenting the complete dissertation.
- Dissertation submission.
- Dissertation defense.

Chapter 4: Conclusion & Future Work

The current research study proposes to implement an online news recommendation system that is more enhanced and improved. The proposed system has been given the alias ONRS, and aims at outperforming the legacy news recommendation systems so as to overcome the pertaining challenges within this domain. To be specific, the proposed system would aim at providing a highly efficient and personalized online news recommendation system to the end-users with a web-interface. The proposed study would build on empirical evidence in order to indulge in practical implementation of the ONRS system. However, considering the time and resource limitations of the proposed study, future research projects may consider large-scale implementation of similar news recommendation systems, while involving major social networks including Facebook, Instagram and Twitter.

References

Agrawal, M., Karimzadehgan, M., & Zhai, C. (2009). An online news recommender system

for social networks. *Urbana, 51*, 61801.

Brafman, R. I., & Tennenholtz, M. (2002). R-max-a general polynomial time algorithm for

near-optimal reinforcement learning. *Journal of Machine Learning Research, 3*(Oct),

213-231.

CSE. (2018). *Reinforcement Learning - Algorithms*. Retrieved 8 January 2018, from

http://www.cse.unsw.edu.au/~cs9417ml/RL1/algorithms.html

Claypool, M., Gokhale, A., Miranda, T., Murnikov, P., Netes, D., & Sartin, M. (1999).

Combing content-based and collaborative filters in an online newspaper. *N.P.*

Chechev, M., Koychev, I. (2014). Recommendations in Social Networks: an Extra Feature or

an Essential Need. In: *Proceedings of MIE 2013, Sofia, Bulgaria (2013)*

Das, A. S., Datar, M., Garg, A., & Rajaram, S. (2007, May). Google news personalization:

scalable online collaborative filtering. In *Proceedings of the 16th international*

conference on World Wide Web (pp. 271-280). ACM.

Elkahky, A. M., Song, Y., & He, X. (2015, May). A multi-view deep learning approach for

cross domain user modeling in recommendation systems. In *Proceedings of the 24th*

International Conference on World Wide Web (pp. 278-288). International World

Wide Web Conferences Steering Committee.

Fung, G., Yu, J., & Lam, W. (2002). News sensitive stock trend prediction. *Advances in*

knowledge discovery and data mining, 481-493.

Garcin, F., Faltings, B., Donatsch, O., Alazzawi, A., Bruttin, C., & Huber, A. (2014,

October). Offline and online evaluation of news recommender systems at swissinfo.

ch. In *Proceedings of the 8th ACM Conference on Recommender systems* (pp. 169-

176). ACM.

Goldberg, K., Roeder, T., Gupta, D., & Perkins, C. (2001). Eigentaste: A constant time collaborative filtering algorithm. *Information Retrieval*, *4*(2), 133-151.

Greenwald, A., Hall, K., & Serrano, R. (2003, August). Correlated Q-learning. In *ICML* (Vol. 3, pp. 242-249).

Hasslet, H.V., Guez, A. & Silver, D. (2016). Deep Reinforcement Learning with Double Q-Learning. *AAAI. 16.*

Hu, J., & Wellman, M. P. (2003). Nash Q-learning for general-sum stochastic games. *Journal of machine learning research*, *4*(Nov), 1039-1069.

Hung, L. P. (2005). A personalized recommendation system based on product taxonomy for one-to-one marketing online. *Expert systems with applications*, *29*(2), 383-392.

Hopfgartner, F., Kille, B., Lommatzsch, A., Plumbaum, T., Brodt, T., & Heintz, T. (2014, September). Benchmarking news recommendations in a living lab. In *International Conference of the Cross-Language Evaluation Forum for European Languages* (pp. 250-267). Springer, Cham.

Hopfgartner, F., Brodt, T., Seiler, J., Kille, B., Lommatzsch, A., Larson, M., ... & Serény, A. (2016, January). Benchmarking news recommendations: The clef newsreel use case. In *ACM SIGIR Forum* (Vol. 49, No. 2, pp. 129-136). ACM.

Lauer, M., & Riedmiller, M. (2000). An algorithm for distributed reinforcement learning in cooperative multi-agent systems. In *In Proceedings of the Seventeenth International Conference on Machine Learning.*

Li, L., Wang, D., Li, T., Knox, D., & Padmanabhan, B. (2011, July). SCENE: a scalable two-stage personalized news recommendation system. In *Proceedings of the 34th international ACM SIGIR conference on Research and development in Information Retrieval* (pp. 125-134). ACM.

Liang, T. P., Lai, H. J., & Ku, Y. C. (2006). Personalized content recommendation and user

satisfaction: Theoretical synthesis and empirical findings. *Journal of Management*

Information Systems, 23(3), 45-70.

Lin, L. J. (1990). Self-improving reactive agents: Case studies of reinforcement learning

frameworks. In *Procs. of the First International Conf. on Simulation of Adaptive*

Behavior: from Animals to Animats, pages 297–305

Liu, J., Dolan, P., & Pedersen, E. R. (2010, February). Personalized news recommendation

based on click behavior. In *Proceedings of the 15th international conference on*

Intelligent user interfaces (pp. 31-40). ACM.

Lu, J., Wu, D., Mao, M., Wang, W., & Zhang, G. (2015). Recommender system application

developments: a survey. *Decision Support Systems, 74*, 12-32.

Merialdo, A. K. B. (1999). Clustering for collaborative filtering applications. *Intelligent*

Image Processing, Data Analysis & Information Retrieval, 3, 199.

Pazzani, M. J., & Billsus, D. (2007). Content-based recommendation systems. In *The*

adaptive web (pp. 325-341). Springer, Berlin, Heidelberg.

Russell, S. J. and Norvig, P. (1995). *Artificial Intelligence: a modern approach.* Prentice-

Hall.

Ribeiro, C. H. C. (1999, July). A tutorial on reinforcement learning techniques. In *Supervised*

Learning Track Tutorials of the 1999 International Joint Conference on Neuronal

Networks.

Shahmohammadi, A., Khadangi, E., & Bagheri, A. (2016). Presenting new collaborative link

prediction methods for activity recommendation in Facebook. *Neurocomputing, 210*,

217-226. doi:10.1016/j.neucom.2016.06.024

Saranya, K. G., & Sadhasivam, G. S. (2012). A personalized online news recommendation

system. *International Journal of Computer Applications, 57*(18).

Shixiang, G., Lillicrap, T., Sutskever, I., & Levine, S. (2016). *Continuous Deep Q-Learning with Model-based Acceleration*. *PMLR*. Retrieved 13 January 2018, from http://proceedings.mlr.press/v48/gu16.html

Xu, Z., Wei, X., Luo, X., Liu, Y., Mei, L., Hu, C., & Chen, L. (2015). Knowle: a semantic link network based system for organizing large scale online news events. *Future Generation Computer Systems*, *43*, 40-50.

YOUR KNOWLEDGE HAS VALUE

- We will publish your bachelor's and master's thesis, essays and papers

- Your own eBook and book - sold worldwide in all relevant shops

- Earn money with each sale

Upload your text at www.GRIN.com
and publish for free